The Ultimate

EFT Tapping Guide for Beginners

Discover How to Use the Emotional Freedom Technique to Accomplish Weight Loss, Conquer Emotional Problems, & Achieve Happiness for Life

Jessica Minty

© Copyright 2014 by Joy Publishing & Marketing Corporation - All rights reserved.

This document is geared towards providing helpful and reliable information in regards to the topic and issue covered. The publication is sold with the idea that the publisher is not required to render accounting, officially permitted, or otherwise, qualified services. If advice is necessary, legal or professional, a practiced individual in the profession should be ordered.

- From a Declaration of Principles which was accepted and approved equally by a Committee of the American Bar Association and a Committee of Publishers and Associations.

In no way is it legal to reproduce, duplicate, or transmit any part of this document in either electronic means or in printed format. Recording of this publication is strictly prohibited and any storage of this document is not allowed unless with written permission from the publisher. All rights reserved.

The information provided herein is stated to be truthful and consistent, in that any liability, in terms of inattention or otherwise, by any usage or abuse of any policies, processes, or directions contained within is the solitary and utter responsibility of the recipient reader. Under no circumstances will any legal responsibility or blame be held against the publisher for any reparation, damages, or monetary loss due to the information herein, either directly or indirectly.

Respective authors own all copyrights not held by the publisher.

The information herein is offered for informational purposes solely, and is universal as so. The presentation of the information is without contract or any type of guarantee assurance.

The trademarks that are used are without any consent, and the publication of the trademark is without permission or backing by the trademark owner. All trademarks and brands within this book are for clarifying purposes only and are the owned by the owners themselves, not affiliated with this document.

Table of Contents

Introduction	*1*
Emotional Freedom Technique: The Basics	*3*
Foundation of EFT Tapping: Your Body's Energy Level	*7*
EFT Tapping	*11*
Tips and Tricks to Make EFT More Effective	*21*
Using EFT Tapping to Address Specific Problems	*27*
Tap Your Way to a Happy Life	*31*
Conclusion	*35*
Preview of Next Book	*37*
Check Out My Other Books	*47*
One Last Thing...	*49*

Introduction

I want to thank you and congratulate you for purchasing this book.

This book contains proven steps and strategies on how to achieve your goals in life using EFT.

This book teaches you how to use EFT Tapping and Affirmation Statements to reach your goals and dreams. It also gives you helpful tips and techniques to take advantage of the benefits of EFT and positive thinking in getting the things you want.

Thanks again for purchasing this book, I hope you enjoy it! Please take some time to stop by and LIKE our Facebook page:

https://www.facebook.com/joypublishing

With gratitude,

Jessica Minty

Emotional Freedom Technique: The Basics

Emotional Freedom Techniques (EFT) is a universal healing tool that helps address physical, performance, and emotional problems. It was developed by Gary Craig, an engineer, in the mid 1990's. He was inspired by the *Thought Filled Therapy* by Dr. Roger Callahan, a psychologist. It operates on the premise that whatever part of your life that you need to improve on, there are unresolved emotional issues in the way.

Backgrounder

EFT is relatively new but it is fast becoming to be a sought after treatment in the field of Energy Psychology. Psychologists often refer to it as "psychological acupressure", a technique used to work on releasing the blockages within the energy system, said to be the source of most of an individual's emotional discomfort. These blockages in the energy system are said to lead people to acquire limited beliefs and behaviors, in addition to challenging an individual emotionally.

However, unlike acupuncture or acupressure, EFT treatments use the fingertips to *tap* on the end points of *energy meridians* that are strategically positioned beneath the skin's surface. EFT has provided relief for a lot of emotional problems and medical conditions, such as, trauma, depression, anxiety, addictions, and physical illnesses.

EFT uses very simple techniques that it can be used as effectively as most self-help tools. It actually helps empower people to be able to actively contribute to their healing process. This fast tracks the healing and relief process.

How Does It Work?

EFT works in the main premise that your negative emotions are caused by the disruption in your energy system. It helps clear the disruptions and eliminate the emotional response.

The process is done by focusing on the particular problem while tapping the corresponding end points of energy meridians with the fingertips. The process is a combination of kinetic energy to your energy system and of uncovering and focusing on the root causes of the problem. It helps facilitate a "straightening out" process to eliminate the sources of the negative emotion or response.

Why Should You Choose EFT?

There are a lot of reasons why you should give EFT a try, here are just some of the feedbacks that you can get when ask actual users:

- This treatment gives you a positive and proactive experience.

- Users and practitioners attest that it actually works where no other treatment can.

- It has a long term effect.

- You can perform some techniques on your own.

- You don't need to purchase any equipment for the treatment.

- You don't need any form of medications or drugs.

- It can be used for weight loss and to overcome addictions.

- It helps you implement positive goals.

- It turns negative emotions into positive.

Improving the More Popular Chinese Treatment

EFT may follow a similar principle with acupuncture and acupressure, but it takes the techniques further by tapping into the emotional issues that are causing your pain or illness. It combines the benefits of acupuncture with the benefits of conventional therapy, this result in a more complete treatment of emotional and physical problems.

Foundation of EFT Tapping: Your Body's Energy Level

EFT is said to help you deal and overcome the following:

- Chronic headaches
- Physical pain
- Stress
- Anxiety and depression
- Fear and panic
- Phobias
- Insomnia
- Grief
- Social anxiety
- Nervousness

It also helps you curb cravings and eventually lose unwanted fats. EFT also improves work performance and provides an excellent personal development technique.

Your Body's Energy System

You've read about the meridian points on the first chapter, the Chinese discovered this complex system of energy circuits running through your entire body some 5,000 years ago. These energy circuits are also called meridians. They are considered to be the centerpiece of the Eastern health practices. They are the very basis of acupressure and acupuncture.

While this energy cannot be seen by the naked eye, you know it's there. It's like the energy that flows through your television set. You realize that it's there because of its effects, the sounds and the images. Tapping into the end points of these energy meridians, you can create a healthier and happier version of yourself.

Western and traditional medical science focus on the chemical nature of the body in relation to the illness and pain it develops. What Western medicine fail to take into account are the subtle yet powerful energy that flows throughout the body.

EFT's Discovery Statement

"The cause of all negative emotions is a disruption in the body's energy system."

This statement sums up the principle behind EFT Tapping. These negative emotions are often cause by the bitter memories of past traumatic experiences. It is imperative to recognize this fact.

Most therapies try to "treat the memory" and makes patients relive these painful experiences. However, the EFT approach is different. It acknowledges the past memories and focuses on the root cause, which is the disruption in the energy system. EFT may let you recall, albeit briefly, a particular painful memory but it doesn't dwell on it.

The traditional method used by most therapies lies in the premise that a particular past traumatic experience is the root cause of the negative emotions that you feel for someone. EFT teaches that it is not because there is a "missing piece" that lies between that particular memory and the emotional upset. There is a disruption in your energy system and this is the direct cause.

Take note that if a painful memory is not caused by a disruption in the energy system, the negative emotion would be non-existent. This is the reason why some people are "haunted" by certain bad memories while others are not. Some people develop an imbalance in their energy system under these painful memories and others do not.

This is where most traditional psychotherapy fails because they focus on the memory instead of the energy disruption. When you are asked to relive a painful memory in the hopes of overcoming them, it only causes further disruption in your energy system. This only means more pain and does not actually address what the real problem is.

EFT zeroes in on the disruption of the energy system with the purpose of restoring its balance within. The internal serenity that you can get from the treatment would help replace the negative emotions, thus providing rapid relief.

EFT Tapping is Like Rebooting Your Computer

The painful memories cause an imbalance in the body's energy system. Your body tells you that it is feeling and thinking about something negative and you it gets stuck there. It's similar to the way your computer gets stuck before the system eventually crashes so you reboot it.

EFT Tapping is similar to rebooting your computer, it is restarting the system. EFT effectively helps you to break free from being stuck and lets you "live" again.

EFT Tapping

EFT Tapping helps clear out the "short circuit" in your body's energy system. It clears the emotional blockage that is causing the imbalance. There are some people who are skeptical about the premise of tapping into the electromagnetic energy flowing throughout the body because of unfamiliarity. This principle is only beginning to get recognized in the West.

EFT Tapping Locations and Technique

There are two basic areas that you need to master to effectively use EFT to create the life that you want; these are the tapping locations and technique, and positive affirmations.

EFT helps release the negative emotions that hinder your growth, success, and happiness. These negative emotions are blockages which come in different forms: stress, anxiety, fear, and frustrations, among others.

The Benefits of Positive Thinking

1. Positive thinking lessens stress and increases energy. Keep in mind that stress wakens you. Stress and anxiety cause you to lose focus. On the other hand, if you think positively, you tap into a hidden energy within yourself that gives you a feeling of lightness.

2. Optimists often outlive pessimists. That's a fact. If you are constantly stressed and anxious, there are medical

conditions that might develop and you fail to live the life you are supposed to enjoy.

3. Positive thinking melts away stress and eventually the physical problems. When you see the positive in every negative situation, you turn it all around and you are able to take advantage of the negative situation instead of "crippling" you.

4. Positive thinking helps improve concentration and focus. If your subconscious mind focuses on terms, like "I can do it" or "Everything is possible", everything will indeed be possible.

5. It gives you more confidence which can contribute to your success. Your strong belief in yourself and your abilities will propel you to greater heights.

Remaining Positive with EFT

While it is hard to remain positive all day long, it is actually doable because of EFT and it can only take a few minutes to change your thinking!

The basic EFT sequence is simple and straightforward. It only takes a few minutes to learn.

Your Fingertips are the Perfect Tools

Instead of using needles, you use your fingertips to tap on the energy meridians. The traditional EFT method uses your index finger and middle finger. You can use either hand for the process. You have to understand that most tapping points are present on either side of your body so you don't have to worry which side you choose.

Another approach is to use all the fingertips of both your hands. The more fingers you use the more it allows access to more pressure points and a larger area can be covered, rather than using two fingertips. You can use either method, one that is more convenient for you.

The fingertips should do the tapping and not the finger pads because the tips contain more meridian points. For those women who like to wear long fingernails, they can use their finger pads instead. In addition, watch and bracelets should be removed prior to the process.

Tap Solidly

Your taps should be solid but you have to take extra care not to hurt yourself.

When using both your hands, experts recommend that tapping movements should be alternating so that each hand is out of phase with the other and not tapping simultaneously. This movement can provide kinesthetic variation which is more beneficial.

When you begin tapping, you will do at least 5 to 7 times. The actual number of taps is not very important, but it should be about the length of a full breath.

You will notice in the list of tapping points below that the meridian points proceed all the way down to the body. Every tapping point is below the one before the last, which should make it easier to remember.

The Right Tapping Points

The following at the correct tapping points that you need to cover every time you perform the treatment. The abbreviations are also indicated.

- *TH – Top of the Head*

Using both hands, your fingers should be back-to-back at the center of the head.

- *EB – Eyebrow*

The points are just above and to each side of the nose, right at the beginning of the eyebrow.

- *SE – Side of the Eye*

The meridian points are right on the bone which is bordering the outside of the corner of each eye.

- *UE – Under the Eye*

It is on the bone just under each eye, which is about an inch below your pupil.

- *UN – Under the Nose*

The points are at the small area located between the bottom of the nose and the top of the upper lip.

- *Ch – Chin*

The meridian points on the chin are midway between the point of your chin and the bottom of the lower lip. Though it is not exactly on the chin, it is referred to as the chin pint for purpose of proper description and easy understanding.

- *CB – Collar Bone*

The points are found at the junction where the breastbone or sternum, the collarbone, and the first rib are connected. This point is a very important point and it is called K27 (kidney) in acupuncture. You can locate the CB point by placing your forefinger on the U-shaped notch found at the top of your breastbone. This is actually where a guy creates a knot on his tie. From the bottom of the U shaped notch, you can move your forefinger down towards your navel (about an inch), and then you move to the right (or left), about an inch.

- *UA – Under the Arm*

The meridian points should be on the side your body, for women, it is in the middle of the bra strap and for men, it should be at the point near the nipple. It is 4 inches below your armpit.

- *WR – Wrists*

This is the last point found inside both your wrists.

The Affirmation Statements

Now that you know how EFT tapping works, the next step is to know what statements to say while you perform the tapping techniques.

Traditional EFT phrase begins with this:

"Even though I have this _____, I deeply and completely accept myself."

This can constitute the second phrase:

"I deeply and completely love and accept myself."

You add to the blank the descriptions of the problem or situation you are struggling with; it can be alcohol or drug addiction, negative emotion, or food cravings.

Examples:

There are a lot issues that can be addressed by EFT tapping techniques:

"Even though I fear speaking in public, I deeply and completely accept myself."

"Even though I have this terrible headache, I deeply and completely accept myself."

"Even though I am suffering from depression and anxiety, I deeply and completely accept myself."

"Even though I have this craving for drugs, I deeply and completely accept myself."

"Even though I have this fear of heights, I deeply and completely accept myself."

"Even though I constantly have nightmares, I deeply and completely accept myself."

You can try other variations to the statements. There is no wrong or right, as long as you follow a similar format: you have to acknowledge the problem and ensure that you create a sincere self-acceptance through your struggles. This is how the affirmation will be effective.

"I love and accept myself even though I am suffering from _____."

or

"I love and accept myself even though I _____."

or

"I continue to accept myself even though I have this _____."

Key Points to Remember

You can use any of the above examples. Just make sure that the statements are easy to remember.

Experts say that is doesn't matter if you believe the affirmation statement or not, say it anyway. Through constant "chants", you will eventually believe every word you say.

The process is made more effective when you deliver the statements with feeling and emphasis, in addition to repeating them daily.

Saying the statement out loud is better, but if you are performing the process where there are other people in the area, you may simply mutter it under your breath, or silently, if you want.

Tuning In

Tuning in to the problem means thinking about the problem. This process will cause energy disruptions and that is the time where balance can be achieved as you make your tapping motions and say your affirmation statement. Without the energy disruptions brought about by *tuning in* to the problem, EFT cannot fully get to work.

The next chapter will give you more ways to take advantage of EFT and the affirmation statements.

Tips and Tricks to Make EFT More Effective

To take advantage of the affirmation statements and EFT tapping techniques, there are a few strategies to know:

The Reminder Phrase

There are instances when a single round of tapping sequence and affirmation statement is enough to get rid of the issue. When subsequent rounds are needed, you can use a *reminder phrase*. This can be a short phrase that you can use to describe the issue you are trying to eliminate and that you will be repeating out loud every time you tap a meridian point in the sequence. This will "remind" your body system about the issue that you are working on.

The most effective reminder phrase that you can use is one that is identical with the affirmation statement you first used; though you can use a shorter version if your initial statement is long. The condensed version should contain a single word or several words to speed the process up a little so you can do more rounds.

For instance, if your issue is to address your fear of public speaking, your initial statement would be:

"Even though I fear speaking in public, I deeply and completely accept myself."

The *"I fear speaking in public"* would be the ideal words to be used in your reminder phrase. Repeating this shortened phrase plus the affirmation can suffice to *tune in* to the issue.

Making Adjustments to the Subsequent Rounds

There are times that a single round of tapping and affirmation may not be enough to eradicate the problem because there are new issues or lingering issues that prevent progress. Whatever these issues are, conversations, images, or interactions, they have something to do, in some ways, with the issue you are currently trying to deal with. This only means that there is more than one issue that hinders you from achieving an excellent well-being. You have to eliminate all of these barriers.

Additional rounds are in order to make sure that all problems are eliminated. You may tweak the affirmation a little to get better results, like this:

"Even though I still have _____, I deeply and completely accept myself."

Take note of the words that were added: *"still"* and *"some"*. They give a different meaning to the affirmation, acknowledging that there issues still exist.

Tips to Consider

- *Be specific* – It is important to use specific terms and languages to make it more effective.

- *Learn to "tune in"* – Tuning in has been discussed in the previous chapter. This is necessary to the process because most of the time, when the issue is emotionally painful, the tendency is to disconnect from these feelings. The reminder phrase will be helpful in this aspect.

- *Be aware of cognitive shifts* – You need to make sure that you are aware of cognitive shifts with every round of the tapping process. A cognitive shift occurs when you look at the issue differently. When you begin to see the issue at a different angle, you begin to see a new insight. This is necessary to the healing process because it might be helpful in opening up new pathways for your complete healing. After every cognitive shift, there is lesser guilt and self-blame. These negative emotions are thereby replaced by a sense of relief or renewed hope.

- *"Through me, not by me"* – When you have a professional therapist helping you with EFT, the healing process is done through the therapist but it is still you who facilitates the healing. EFT practitioners are merely facilitators and instruments for the process; you still heal yourself through their help.

- *Make sure you are properly hydrated* – Water is a conductor of electricity and the treatment accesses the electrical energy from your body and your mind. Make sure you and the EFT practitioner assisting you are properly hydrated.

Practicing Your Affirmation Statements

Affirmation statements help improve the effects of EFT. Positive self-statements are helpful. Make sure they are definitive. These statements may not be true at first, you will have to say them anyway, and through constant repetitions, they would influence the way think and feel and eventually get rid of the issue you wish to address.

Timing is Important

To make your affirmations more effective, it is important that you say them in the morning when you wake up, before you go to bed, or even when you go to the bathroom. For the tapping movements, the best time to do them plus the affirmations is before going to sleep. EFT practitioners say that this is the single most important time to do the routine. Tapping before you sleep helps give your subconscious at least 6 to 8 hours to process the affirmations and help make them a reality for you.

Most practitioners also recommend finding a prayer that you can integrate to your EFT routines as this may increase the affirmations' efficiency.

Once you have your affirmations ready and learned the important tapping points, you can start doing them.

A Mirror Can Come in Handy

You only need a mirror to do this. You might find it more effective to tap as you stare at your own eyes, while you are in front of a mirror. Experts say that this can give you a deeper connection with your subconscious mind. You are actually using the mirror to reflect back the energy into you, instead of going out into space.

This is simple yet practitioners attest to its effectiveness.

Looking into your own reflection in the mirror while doing tapping sequences and saying those positive affirmations lets you see if you are tapping on the right points. Make sure that you pay attention to what you are saying and hearing. Do not focus on negative messages that might block your progress.

Try this powerful technique and see for yourself how effective it can be. For example, you can try this affirmation as you tap and look into your eyes:

"Even though I was impatient, I forgive you; I was just trying to do the best I could. I forgive you for holding onto these negative thoughts and patterns for a long time."

Note that as you say the words, *"I forgive you"* look into your eyes. Always acknowledge the negative feelings and thoughts, especially if you know they are there, but don't dwell on them. Let EFT turn those negatives into positives.

Using EFT Tapping to Address Specific Problems

Why You Can't Achieve Your Goals?

One of the most common issues that present itself when you begin tapping to minimize food cravings so you can lose weight is when you have memories of an image, place, or person that the cravings remind you of. As you perform tapping sequences, you have to take extra care in paying attention to these negative thoughts that might come up. Listen, as well, to any statements from your subconscious.

These negative thoughts hinder you to move forward with EFT and prevent you from achieving your goal. Unless you are able to address these issues directly, you will not be able to achieve your goals of losing weight or achieving inner, or whatever it is that you wish to address.

The solution is easy. As you use EFT, you have to acknowledge whatever these self-critical thoughts may be, and then, you have to love and accept yourself again as you tap on your meridian points.

The real issue is not really the food cravings, it is actually the love and attention you need from someone, like your mom or your dad, that you didn't get, it made you sad and/or upset. You then resorted to eat cake or anything you can get your hands on to compensate for the attention that you didn't get. This may be categorized as emotional eating.

The subconscious has a lot of power but you can use EFT to turn the negative thoughts and feelings it might try to instill in your conscious mind by replacing them with positive thoughts and feelings.

How You Can Tap Your Way to Achieving Your Goals

The *inquiry process* is a helpful tool in uncovering the unconscious blockages that hinder you from getting the results you want. This is an excellent tool to help you discover the thoughts, feelings, and images that might be de-motivating you in pursuing the things you want to achieve.

Remember that your conscious mind states your goals but it is from the subconscious mind that thoughts and ideas begin. So, when there are things that you want to achieve, yet, whatever you do, you cannot seem to achieve them, there might be a disconnect on your subconscious. You might not be using its power.

- *Uncovering Unconscious Blocks*

For instance, if you want to lose weight, put into writing the exact weight you want to lose. You have to make sure that you are clear and specific with your goals. This will be your conscious intention.

When you have established your conscious intention and stated them, negative thoughts and feeling might begin to set in. These blockages significantly bar you from achieving your goal. You might think of statements like, *"Achieving my weight loss goal is difficult and I have a really long way to go"* or *"It takes a lot of hard work, I don't know how I can go about it"*, might begin to reign in your subconscious.

Rate the negative thoughts from 1 to 10, with 10 being the most intense or true. You will be revisiting that ranking once you are done with several rounds of tapping sequences. The goal is to bring down the rating.

- *Releasing those Unconscious Blocks*

As mentioned in the first chapter, your body has meridian or energy points that you can stimulate. You can tap on these meridian points and release the negative feelings and emotions. For a beginner, you can create a tapping script similar to this:

Side of the hand: *"Even though I have much to do, I'm tired, and overwhelmed, I love and accept myself."* (Repeat this statement at least 3 times.)

Inner eye: *"I have too much to do."*

Outer eye: *"I just cannot do everything at the same time."*

Under eye: *"It will be a long hill climb for me to lose weight."*

Upper lip: *"It's a lot of work."*

Chin: *"I am too overwhelmed and I can't find in my busy schedule to do other things."*

Collar bone: *"You cannot make me do one more thing."*

Side of the body: *"I am just too overwhelmed."*

Top of the head: *"This is going to be hard and I know I can't do it."*

Repeat the above sequence until you feel that things begin to shift. Now, use these variations:

Inner eye: *"What if it isn't that hard?"*

Outer eye: *"What if it will be easy?"*

Under eye: *"What if you find it fun."*

Upper lip: *"What if you'll be inspired?"*

Chin: *"What if it would be energizing?"*

Collar bone: *"What if losing weight is not about working for it but letting it all go?"*

Side of the body: *"What if you only need to feel and accept the feelings?"*

Top of the head: *"I love and accept myself and all that I am feeling right now."*

The process is actually about discovering the subconscious blockages hindering you from achieving your goals. The process can give you the energy you need, rather than overwhelming you and causing you more stress as you release these trapped emotions from your subconscious. You allow yourself to be open to more positive beliefs and other favorable possibilities.

Tap Your Way to a Happy Life

Who doesn't want to have a happy life? While it is a known fact that life is not a bed of roses, you can still feel good even if you don't own a fancy sports car or live in a huge mansion. Therapists say that people have to learn to be happy in the simplest of things. A good and meaningful life is not achieved by owning material things or having a stellar career alone.

You can be the richest person in the world but still remain unhappy. As you come to the end of this book, you begin to realize that everything begins from your subconscious. Feelings of elation are transient. After the initial electrical stimulation, the nerve impulses begin to fade. Material rewards are not reliably the bearer of good feelings. When you are able to discover a more permanent source of happiness, you can say that you live a happy life.

Your Emotions Set the Context

You now know that your mind is full of memories from all your past experiences. Every living moment, there is a corresponding emotion that dominates your mind. You cannot control what comes into your life but you can control how you react to them, by directing your subconscious to turn those negative feelings into positive. Feeling good is staying away from negative emotions.

EFT Tapping Helps

Negative emotions will only fill you with more resentment and anxiety and EFT will help negate these negative emotions. Note that each person is vulnerable to habitual patterns of negative thoughts. When the emotional turmoil within yourself is eliminated, you begin to feel the real calmness.

As you begin to change your frame of mind, you also begin to view problems, issues, and challenges as non-threatening to your inner peace. They simply become incident possibilities.

Freedom from the Negative Brings You Joy

Once you free yourself from the negative emotions and feelings that has been blocking happiness and inner peace, you begin to feel unbounded joy and happiness. Keep in mind that a new sports car can only make you feel euphoric for some time. The happiness you feel when you have acquired your dream house is also temporary. Good feelings from material things do not persist but the good feeling that you get from the inside stays forever. Mindfulness living is your key to a happy and contented life.

Mindfulness is just what you need to fully appreciate the goodness of life. Sure, it is not wrong to aspire to own material things, these will be your rewards for working hard, but your happiness is not tied to fame and fortune, happiness should come from within yourself.

The Way to Be Happy

Not every person can own a mansion or a fancy car. Do not dwell on the popular notions of desirable satisfactions. EFT

Tapping can help save you from stressing over achieving unrealistic goals. You are unique in your own way, with talents and gifts that you can use to achieve the goals that you want to achieve. You may get the same opportunity the man in the White House has but you can still become great in your own way. You can still be happy wherever you are; happiness is a state of mind!

Conclusion

Thank you again for purchasing this book!

I hope this book was able to help you to live the happy life you have been longing for.

The next step is to put the techniques you have learned into practice and share your knowledge with your family and friends.

Finally, please remember to check out our Facebook page in order to find other resources and upcoming promotions:

https://www.facebook.com/joypublishing

With sincere thanks,

Jessica Minty

Preview of "Mindfulness Meditation Guide: The Key to Building Willpower, Escalating Happiness and Conquering Stress"

Chapter 1

The Basics of Mindfulness: Discovering What Your Mind Can Do

The famous saying "What your mind can conceive, your body can achieve" has been extensively used in order to motivate people to pursue whatever their goal is. This is because if their mind is set on a single goal, the body will be directed as to what actions must be taken to achieve it. Fortunately, this saying is also applicable in helping us cope with problems and invite positive vibes in our life.

This chapter aims to discover the basics of mindfulness – what it is, and how its practice can lead to a better life.

What is mindfulness?

Mindfulness is a form of meditation which aims to become aware of your feelings, sensations, and thoughts while you are in a non-judgmental and relaxed state. In a simpler sense, its aim is to know what's going on with your self internally and in the present moment. When a person is mindful, they are able to see everything around them naturally, and are not concerned with what or how things should be.

Mindfulness is said to be similar to a Buddhist meditation practiced that was started around 2500 years ago. However, mindfulness is not a religiously connected meditation method, and every person regardless of their religious affiliation can practice it.

A majority of the time, our brain functions on auto pilot when we go about our daily actions. This is a very efficient tool that the brain uses. However, so often we find ourselves behaving in ways that don't line up with what we value. I'm constantly caught in the trap of where I know I want to be and what I'm actually doing in the present moment. I get so frustrated with myself when my behaviors don't line up with my values. Why is it that I want to do "good", but I can't? When I don't want to do "bad," I do it anyway? How annoying this cycle is for me.

Fortunately, the brain is smart and knows that it doesn't always get it right. That's why it give us consciousness so we can interrupt the process and turn off the auto pilot. Mindfulness is actually the key to turning the auto pilot off and enhancing your ability to recognize what your brain is doing.

There are so many fantastic benefits to mindfulness meditation. This is actually a really exciting time for mindfulness and science. Research on the incredibleness of mindfulness is increasing rapidly because scientists are realizing how pivotal mindfulness is on our brain health. It won't be long before mindfulness sky rockets through the population and everyone will be doing it. It's kind of like how yoga became popular and little yoga studios popped up everywhere. In the same way, I believe that mindfulness will be taught in schools and there will also be studios popping up around the city. It will become common place, as it should.

Could you imagine if they actually taught this stuff in school? I'm a teacher so I get really fired up about this. I teach practical life skills to my students and now where in the curriculum is such a beneficial and life altering skill taught. If people were educated on how to deal with stress, anger, depression, cravings, etc, our world would be such a different place. Ooooh, it gets me excited at the possibilities of what could be. That's why this book is so important to me.

So what are its benefits?

The following benefits can be experienced by people who practice mindfulness:

- It can help lower stress – applying mindfulness in daily situations has been found to lower stress. When a person is in the state of mindfulness, they are more able to determine the root cause of their problem. It will also help them to prioritize which problem should be attended to first. As their mind becomes open to their problems without negative thoughts, better solutions can be conceived. Ultimately, this will lead to solving the whole problem.

- It can help prevent depression and anxiety – some people are easily overwhelmed when they are faced with problems that seem to stack one after another. As you are able to prioritize which problems should be solved first by applying mindfulness, the feeling that you can't get over them will eventually fade away. Similarly, the feeling of depression is also reduced. After all, the more control you have with the situation, the less anxious and the more emotionally stable you are.

- It can help improve your physical health – it is common for meditation methods to include relaxation techniques. Deep breathing and getting calm, some of the behaviors observed in meditation methods, are known to improve heart rate and lower blood pressure.

- It can improve your memory and mental functions – surprisingly, mindfulness can also enhance a person's memory. This is because mindfulness requires you to recall every possible situation that you've experienced during the day. You are also forced to think of every possible solution to situations that are causing you problems. As you use your brain more, your mental function will improve as well. The process of mindfulness actually rewires the brain. Studies on the brain show incredible improvements to the brain in as short as two weeks!

- It helps you see the situation on a new light – even the worst possible situation that you can ever think of has a silver lining. Either there is a meaning behind it, or there is a lesson that you can learn from it. With the help of mindfulness, it becomes easier to see the problem in another perspective. This in turn will help you to become more positive in dealing with the problem and avoid having negative feelings about it.

- It curbs your cravings – mindfulness practices have been used to control food cravings and even strong emotions. The SOBER technique, which will be shared later, is a fantastic technique that comes out on top through research studies on cravings.

- It builds self confidence and self acceptance – mindfulness notices our thoughts for what they are: neutral. There are no "good" or "bad" thoughts. Just thoughts. The problem is when we show up and attach meaning to those thoughts. But mindfulness just lets those thoughts float through our mind and not attach meaning to them. As quickly as those thoughts come is as quickly as they leave. I found this concept profound and it really clicked with me. Many years ago, when I was wrestling with postpartum depression, I learned about this concept in counseling. I so often would have bombarding thoughts that would go through my mind that I associated as negative. As a result, I would beat myself up for having those thoughts and label myself in negative ways. However, when I learned that I can just let my thoughts pass through my mind without having any attachment to who I was as a person – I was set free! What a relief for me. I continue to practice this concept to this day.

- It enhances willpower – willpower is a key factor in the quality and length of our life. It behaves like a muscle that needs to get exercised in order to grow bigger. We all know that our lives would be so much more successful if we actually did the behaviors that we know we should. More often than not, we don't because we aren't disciplined enough to follow through. Consequently, we've developed a habit of not doing rather than a habit of doing. Mindfulness meditation is one of the best ways that you can drastically improve your willpower. Research studies show that the improvements to our brain are almost instantaneous! Chapter 3 continues talking about willpower and I have a book dedicated to it: "Willpower Guide."

- It increases your heart rate variability – your heart rate variability is connected with your willpower. Science is also zeroing in its affects in our body. So far, we know that our heart rate variability communicates how much willpower is at our disposal. Obviously, the wider our heart rate variability, the better our willpower will be. Meditation is one of the best methods for enhancing your heart rate variability. The effects in studies are shown to be almost immediate. Again, I talk more about heart rate variability, and what to do/not do in "Willpower Guide." Another resource for you to use is www.heartmath.org. You just need to type in "heart rate variability" into their search engine.

Why mindfulness is not that easy?

Since mindfulness shares the same practices observed in other meditation techniques, you might think that it is not that difficult to apply. This belief, however, is false. This is because the following issues are experienced by people who practice mindfulness:

- Some of your expectations may not be met – people who start applying mindfulness meditation usually have low expectations at first. But as they continue to engage in this activity for quite some time, their expectation of the occurrence of results increases. After all, they've given enough time and opportunity for this method to show results, and it is natural for people to expect results from something that they've spent their time on. Unfortunately, mindfulness is not similar to prescription medicine, since it never gives results immediately. Even if the goal of mindfulness is to provide the benefits stated above, there is no definite schedule as to when its effects will be experienced. If expectations are not met, there is a huge tendency that the person will stop meditating, with the belief that this method "does not work". Although you may not yet see changes, know that your brain and heart chemistry immediately react, as proven by scans during research.

- Its practice can make you feel uncomfortable – when a person starts meditation, they can either be physically uncomfortable, or their thoughts may cause them discomfort.

a. Being physically uncomfortable – in this form of meditation, you are required to remain in a seated position or in other comfortable position. However, getting uncomfortable cannot be avoided, especially if you have to maintain the said position for a significant amount of time. Although being aware of what your body is experiencing can be a part of the routine, these issues can be significant enough and may interrupt your meditation.

b. Getting uncomfortable with your thoughts – when a person is not in motion, his or her mind will bring into consciousness different ideas or thoughts. Although having more of these thoughts are beneficial in formulating solutions to your problems, the surge of ideas can also create more confusion as to which is the best solution for your problem. Simply put, it can slow down their pace when making decisions. There will also be instances when undesirable thoughts surface as the meditation continues, which can become distracting if they follow through it. And even if the meditation was stopped due to the continuous re-surfacing of the undesirable thought, the fact that it was brought into awareness can make it difficult for you to forget about it. There is a risk that you'll be adding another problem that you have to solve.

Although it can be hard to start, it's important to start. Habits take at least 21 days to form. This is definitely a habit you want to form! Start small on a daily basis. Begin with 3 minutes and work your way up to 10 or 15 minutes or longer. Don't beat yourself up if you are unable to commit to 10 – 15 minutes. It is better to have a short meditation practice than none at all. You will still acquire the profound benefits.

Check out the rest of this book on Amazon

Or go to: http://amzn.to/1vDwDTS

Check Out My Other Books

Below you'll find some of my other books also available:

Anxiety Relief: Anxiety Management & Stress Solutions for Overcoming Anxiety, Worry & Dread to Emotional Health, Anxiety Free & Stress Relief

Codependency: A Relationship Rescue for Toxic Relationships, Manipulation & Enabling to Self Confidence, Boundaries, Emotional Health & Happiness ****BEST SELLER****

EFT Tapping: Emotional Freedom to Break Free From Cravings, Temptation & Bad Habits to Emotional Health, Stress Relief & Happiness

Jealousy: A Relationship Rescue for Overcoming Fear, Insecurity, Trust Issues, Lying & Envy to Trust & Healthy Relationships

Manipulation: A Relationship Rescue for Breaking Free from Bad Relationships, Mind Control, Emotional Abuse & Codependency to Reclaiming Your Self Confidence & Sanity

Mindfulness Meditation: Mindfulness & Anxiety Management for Overcoming Anxiety & Worry to Emotional Health, Inner Peace & Happiness

Perfectionism: Letting Go of Mistakes & Overcoming Anxiety, Perfection & Procrastination to Victory & Self Acceptance

Self Confidence: Breaking Free from Shyness, Insecurity & Shame to Self Care, Self Acceptance & Self Esteem

Willpower: Breaking Free From Cravings, Temptation & Bad Habits to Self Control, Self Discipline & Goal Setting

One Last Thing...

Source: Wikipedia

If you believe that this book is worth sharing, would you please take the time to let others know how it affected your life? If it turns out to make a difference in the lives of others, they will be forever grateful to you, as will I.

Made in the USA
Columbia, SC
01 May 2025